An Introduction to Statistics

A Comprehensive Guide

copyrighted@2023

Modella Michelle

Table of Contents

Chapter One

An Introduction to Statistics
Understanding the Basics

1.1 What is Statistics?

Statistics is a branch of mathematics and a powerful tool used to gather, organize, analyze, interpret, and present data. It deals with the collection, presentation, analysis, and interpretation of numerical information to draw meaningful conclusions and make informed decisions. Statistics is widely used in various fields such as business, economics, medicine, psychology, social sciences, engineering, and more.

1.2 Importance of Statistics in Various Fields

Statistics plays a crucial role in many aspects of modern life. It enables researchers, scientists, and policymakers to:

- Make Informed Decisions: Statistics helps in understanding trends, patterns, and relationships within data, allowing for well-informed decisions.

- Test Hypotheses: By using statistical tests, researchers can validate or reject hypotheses based on data.

- Predict and Forecast: Statistical methods like time series analysis and regression enable forecasting future trends and outcomes.

- Analyze Risk and Uncertainty: Statistics aids in risk assessment and quantifying uncertainty through probability models.

- Conduct Surveys: In fields such as market research, social sciences, and public opinion studies, statistics helps in designing and interpreting surveys.

- Evaluate Interventions: Statistical analysis is used to assess the impact of interventions and treatments in medical and social research.

1.3 Types of Data: Categorical and Numerical

Data can be categorized into two main types: categorical and numerical.

- Categorical Data: This type of data represents categories or groups. Examples include gender (male/female), colors, marital status, and types of animals. Categorical data can further be divided into nominal (non-ordered categories) and ordinal (ordered categories) data.

- Numerical Data: Numerical data consists of numbers and can be further divided into two subtypes:

  - Discrete Data: These are whole numbers representing counts, such as the number of students in a class.

  - Continuous Data: These are real numbers representing measurements, such as height, weight, or temperature.

1.4 Populations and Samples

- Population: The population refers to the entire group or set of individuals or items that we are interested in studying. For example, if we want to study the heights of all adults in a country, the entire adult population of that country would be our population.

- Sample: A sample is a smaller subset of the population that is selected for observation or analysis. It is often impractical or impossible to study an entire population, so a well-chosen sample can provide useful information about the entire population.

1.5 Descriptive vs. Inferential Statistics

- Descriptive Statistics: Descriptive statistics involves organizing, summarizing, and presenting data to describe the main features of a dataset. Measures of central tendency (mean, median, mode), measures of variability (range, variance, standard deviation), and graphical representations (bar charts, histograms) are examples of descriptive statistics.

- Inferential Statistics: Inferential statistics involves making inferences or predictions about a population based on data collected from a sample. It includes hypothesis testing, confidence intervals, and regression analysis. Inferential statistics allows researchers to draw conclusions and make generalizations beyond the observed sample.

Subsequently, we will delve deeper into various statistical techniques, methods of data analysis, and their applications to gain a better understanding of the role of statistics in decision making and problem-solving.

Data Collection and Sampling

2.1 Data Sources: Primary vs. Secondary

Data collection is a fundamental step in the statistical process. There are two main sources of data:

- Primary Data: Primary data is collected directly from the source or through firsthand observation. This involves designing surveys, experiments, or conducting interviews and questionnaires to gather specific information. Primary data is original and tailored to the research objectives, making it more relevant and reliable for the study.

- Secondary Data: Secondary data is collected by someone else for a different purpose but can be used for a new study. It includes data from published sources, government reports, research papers, and online databases. While secondary data can save time and resources, researchers should critically evaluate its quality and relevance to ensure it aligns with their research objectives.

2.2 Sampling Techniques: Random, Stratified, Systematic, Cluster

Sampling is the process of selecting a subset (sample) from a larger population to represent the entire group. Proper sampling ensures that the sample accurately reflects the characteristics of the population.

There are various sampling techniques:

- Random Sampling: In random sampling, each member of the population has an equal chance of being selected. This technique ensures unbiased representation of the population and is commonly used when conducting surveys or experiments.

- Stratified Sampling: Stratified sampling involves dividing the population into subgroups or strata based on certain characteristics (e.g., age, gender, income), and then selecting a random sample from each stratum. This technique ensures representation from each subgroup, making it useful when there are significant variations within the population.

- Systematic Sampling: In systematic sampling, researchers select every nth individual from the population. The first individual is chosen randomly, and subsequent selections follow a fixed pattern. This method is straightforward and efficient when a complete list of the population is available.

- Cluster Sampling: Cluster sampling involves dividing the population into clusters or groups and then randomly selecting some clusters for the sample. All members within the chosen clusters are included in the sample. This method is suitable when it is impractical or expensive to sample individuals directly.

2.3 Bias and Sampling Errors

Bias in sampling refers to a systematic error that occurs when the sample is not representative of the population. It leads to inaccurate or misleading results. Several types of biases can affect sampling:

- Selection Bias: Occurs when certain individuals or groups have a higher chance of being included or excluded from the sample due to the sampling method or non-response.

- Measurement Bias: Arises when there are inaccuracies in the data collection process, such as poorly worded survey questions or biased observers.

- Non-Response Bias: Occurs when some selected individuals in the sample do not participate or respond to the data collection, leading to an incomplete representation of the population.

Sampling errors are inherent in any sampling process and refer to the discrepancies between the sample statistic and the true population parameter. They occur due to chance and can be reduced by increasing the sample size.

2.4 Sample Size Determination

The size of the sample directly influences the reliability and precision of the study's results. Determining an appropriate sample size depends on several factors, including:

- Desired Level of Confidence: The level of confidence indicates the certainty researchers want to have in their results. Common confidence levels are 95% or 99%.

- Margin of Error: The margin of error is the maximum allowable difference between the sample estimate and the population parameter. Smaller margins of error require larger sample sizes.

- Variability of the Population: When the population is highly variable, a larger sample size is needed to capture its characteristics accurately.

- Cost and Time Constraints: Larger sample sizes may be costlier and more time-consuming to collect and analyze.

Statistical techniques, such as power analysis, can aid in determining an appropriate sample size to achieve the desired level of accuracy and precision for the study.

In the next chapter, we will explore descriptive statistics, which involves organizing and summarizing the collected data to gain insights and understand its main features. Proper data collection and sampling are critical for obtaining reliable and meaningful statistical results.

Descriptive Statistics

3.1 Measures of Central Tendency: Mean, Median, Mode

Measures of central tendency are used to describe the typical or central value of a dataset. They help us understand the average or most representative value. The main measures of central tendency are:

- Mean: The mean is the arithmetic average of all the values in a dataset. It is calculated by adding up all the values and dividing the sum by the number of observations. The mean is sensitive to extreme values (outliers).

- Median: The median is the middle value when the data is arranged in ascending or descending order. If there is an even number of observations, the median is the average of the two middle values. The median is robust to extreme values and is often used when dealing with skewed datasets.

- Mode: The mode is the value that appears most frequently in the dataset. A dataset can have one mode (unimodal), two modes (bimodal), or more (multimodal).

Some datasets may have no mode if all values are unique.

3.2 Measures of Variability: Range, Variance, Standard Deviation

Measures of variability indicate the spread or dispersion of data points around the central tendency. They help assess how much the data deviates from the average. The main measures of variability are:

- Range: The range is the difference between the maximum and minimum values in the dataset. It gives a basic idea of the data's spread but is sensitive to extreme values.

- Variance: The variance measures the average squared deviation from the mean. It provides a more precise measure of dispersion than the range but is less interpretable as it is in squared units.

- Standard Deviation: The standard deviation is the square root of the variance. It is one of the most widely used measures of variability as it is in the same units as the original data. A larger standard deviation indicates more variability in the data.

3.3 Skewness and Kurtosis

Skewness and kurtosis are measures that assess the shape of the data distribution.

- Skewness: Skewness measures the asymmetry of the dataset. Positive skewness indicates that the tail is elongated to the right (right-skewed) and the mean is greater than the median. Negative skewness indicates a left-skewed distribution with a longer tail to the left of the peak.

- Kurtosis: Kurtosis measures the peakedness or flatness of the data distribution. A normal distribution has a kurtosis of 3, which is called mesokurtic. Kurtosis greater than 3 indicates a more peaked distribution (leptokurtic), while kurtosis less than 3 indicates a flatter distribution (platykurtic).

3.4 Percentiles and Quartiles

Percentiles and quartiles divide a dataset into equal parts and provide valuable information about its distribution.

- Percentiles: Percentiles represent the values below which a given percentage of the data falls. For example, the 25th percentile is the value below which 25% of the data lies.

- Quartiles: Quartiles are specific percentiles that divide the data into four equal parts. The first quartile (Q1) is the 25th percentile, the second quartile (Q2) is the median, and the third quartile (Q3) is the 75th percentile.

3.5 Frequency Distributions and Histograms

Frequency distributions are tables that organize data into groups or intervals and display the frequency of observations falling within each group. Histograms are graphical representations of frequency distributions, where the data is presented as bars on a continuous scale. Histograms help visualize the shape and pattern of the data distribution, especially in large datasets.

Descriptive statistics provide a snapshot of the dataset's main characteristics, aiding in summarizing data and gaining insights into its underlying structure. In the next chapter, we will explore data visualization techniques, which complement descriptive statistics in presenting data in a more visually appealing and informative manner.

Chapter Two

Data Visualization

4.1 Graphical Representation of Data

Data visualization is the graphical representation of data to facilitate the understanding of patterns, trends, and insights that might be hidden in raw data. Visualizations make it easier for humans to comprehend complex information, identify outliers, and communicate findings effectively.

4.2 Bar Charts and Pie Charts

- Bar Charts: Bar charts are one of the most common types of graphs used to display categorical data. They consist of vertical or horizontal bars, with the length of each bar representing the frequency or count of a category. Bar charts are useful for comparing the relative sizes of different categories.

- Pie Charts: Pie charts display the proportion of each category as a slice of a circular chart. The size of each slice corresponds to the percentage of the total data it represents. Pie charts are effective for illustrating part-to-whole relationships.

4.3 Scatter Plots and Line Graphs

- Scatter Plots: Scatter plots are used to display the relationship between two numerical variables. Each data point is represented by a dot, with its position on the graph determined by the values of the two variables. Scatter plots help identify patterns, correlations, or clusters in the data.

- Line Graphs: Line graphs show the relationship between two numerical variables over a continuous range. The data points are connected by lines, which help visualize trends and changes over time or along a continuous scale.

4.4 Box Plots and Whisker Diagrams

- Box Plots: Box plots, also known as box-and-whisker plots, display the distribution of numerical data. The box represents the interquartile range (IQR), with the median line inside it. The whiskers extend to the minimum and maximum values within a certain range or outliers beyond the range.

- Whisker Diagrams: Whisker diagrams are an extension of box plots, used to visualize the distribution of data in multiple groups or categories side by side. They are helpful in comparing distributions and identifying differences between groups.

4.5 The Role of Visualization in Data Analysis

Data visualization plays a vital role in the data analysis process:

- Exploratory Data Analysis: Visualizations help analysts explore data, spot patterns, identify outliers, and form hypotheses about relationships between variables.

- Communication of Findings: Visualizations aid in presenting data insights to stakeholders in a clear and understandable manner, enhancing decision-making processes.

- Data Validation: Visualizations help in detecting errors or inconsistencies in data, ensuring data quality and accuracy.

- Pattern Recognition: Visualizations make it easier to recognize trends, clusters, or anomalies in large datasets, which might be challenging to identify through numerical analysis alone.

- Predictive Modeling: Visualizations assist in understanding the relationships between variables and selecting relevant features for predictive modeling.

4.6 Advanced Visualization Techniques

In addition to the basic visualizations mentioned above, advanced techniques include:

- Heatmaps: Heatmaps represent data using color intensity to visualize patterns in matrices or tables.

- Geographic Maps: Geographic maps plot data on geographical locations, making spatial patterns easily recognizable.

- Treemaps: Treemaps display hierarchical data using nested

rectangles, with each level representing a category.

- Bubble Charts: Bubble charts represent data points with circles, with the size of each circle indicating an additional data dimension.

- 3D Visualization: 3D plots add depth to the visualizations, suitable for examining relationships in three-dimensional datasets.

Data visualization tools and libraries, such as Matplotlib, Seaborn, ggplot2, and Tableau, simplify the creation of visualizations and enable interactive and dynamic data exploration.

Probability Theory

5.1 Understanding Probability

Probability is a branch of mathematics that deals with the likelihood of events occurring. In the context of statistics, probability plays a crucial role in quantifying uncertainty and randomness. Probability is expressed as a value between 0 and 1, where 0 indicates an impossible event, and 1 represents a certain event.

5.2 Probability Rules: Addition and Multiplication Rules

- Addition Rule: The addition rule states that the probability of either event A or event B occurring is the sum of their individual probabilities, minus the probability of both events occurring simultaneously (if they are not mutually exclusive):

$$P(A \cup B) = P(A) + P(B) - P(A \cap B)$$

- Multiplication Rule: The multiplication rule states that the probability of both event A and event B occurring is the product of their individual probabilities, given that they are independent events:

$$P(A \cap B) = P(A) * P(B) \quad \text{(if A and B are independent)}$$

5.3 Conditional Probability

Conditional probability measures the probability of an event occurring given that another event has already occurred. It is denoted by $P(A \mid B)$, read as "the probability of A given B." The formula for conditional probability is:

$$P(A \mid B) = P(A \cap B) / P(B)$$
$$\text{(assuming } P(B) > 0)$$

5.4 Bayes' Theorem

Bayes' Theorem is a fundamental concept in probability theory and is used to update the probability of an event based on new evidence. It is especially valuable in the field of statistical inference and decision-making. The theorem can be expressed as:

$$P(A \mid B) = \frac{P(B \mid A) * P(A)}{P(B)}$$

Where:

- P(A | B) is the posterior probability (the probability of event A given evidence B).

- P(B | A) is the likelihood (the probability of evidence B given event A).

- P(A) is the prior probability (the initial probability of event A before considering evidence B).

- P(B) is the marginal likelihood (the probability of evidence B occurring).

5.5 Probability Distributions: Discrete and Continuous

Probability distributions describe the probabilities of different outcomes in a random experiment. There are two main types of probability distributions:

- Discrete Probability Distribution: In a discrete distribution, the random variable takes on distinct and separate values. The probabilities are represented as a probability mass function (PMF). Examples of discrete distributions include the binomial, Poisson, and geometric distributions.

- Continuous Probability Distribution: In a continuous distribution, the random variable can take any value within a certain range. The probabilities are represented as a probability density function (PDF). Examples of continuous distributions include the normal (Gaussian), exponential, and uniform distributions.

Probability distributions play a crucial role in inferential statistics, where they are used to model data and make predictions about populations based on sample observations.

Understanding probability theory is essential for statistical analysis, hypothesis testing, and decision-making. In the subsequent chapters, we will explore common probability distributions and their applications in various statistical analyses.

Common Probability Distributions

Probability distributions describe the likelihood of different outcomes in a random experiment or event. In statistical analysis, understanding and using common probability distributions are essential for making predictions, estimating parameters, and conducting hypothesis testing.

6.1 The Normal Distribution

The normal distribution, also known as the Gaussian distribution, is one of the most important and widely used probability distributions. It is characterized by a symmetric bell-shaped curve. The normal distribution is fully defined by its mean (μ) and standard deviation (σ).

Many natural phenomena and measurement errors follow a normal distribution, making it a fundamental concept in statistics. Central Limit Theorem states that the sampling distribution of the mean of a sufficiently large sample from any population will be approximately normally distributed.

6.2 The Binomial Distribution

The binomial distribution is a discrete probability distribution that describes the number of successes in a fixed number of independent Bernoulli trials (experiments with only two possible outcomes: success or failure). The distribution is characterized by two parameters: the number of trials (n) and the probability of success on each trial (p).

The binomial distribution is useful in situations where outcomes are binary, such as counting the number of heads in a series of coin tosses or the number of successes in a series of independent yes/no questions.

6.3 The Poisson Distribution

The Poisson distribution is a discrete probability distribution used to model the number of events that occur in a fixed interval of time or space when events are rare and independent. It is characterized by a single parameter λ (lambda), which represents the average rate of events occurring in the given interval.

The Poisson distribution is applicable in scenarios such as modeling the number of customers arriving at a store in an hour or the number of defects in a manufacturing process.

6.4 The Exponential Distribution

The exponential distribution is a continuous probability distribution that models the time between successive events in a Poisson process (a process where events occur at a constant rate and independently). It is characterized by a parameter λ (lambda), which represents the rate parameter or the average number of events per unit of time.

The exponential distribution is used in reliability analysis, queuing theory, and survival analysis, where it models the time to failure of a device, the time between customer arrivals, or the time until an event occurs.

6.5 Other Important Distributions

There are several other important probability distributions used in statistics:

- Uniform Distribution: The uniform distribution is a continuous distribution where all outcomes are equally likely within a given range. It is often used in random number generation and in scenarios where all possibilities have the same likelihood.

- Gamma Distribution: The gamma distribution is a continuous distribution that extends the exponential distribution to handle more general shapes. It is often used in modeling wait times and queuing systems.

- Chi-Square Distribution: The chi-square distribution is a continuous distribution that arises in the context of hypothesis testing, particularly when dealing with categorical data.

- Student's t-Distribution: The t-distribution is a continuous distribution used in hypothesis testing when the sample size is small or when the population standard deviation is unknown.

- F-Distribution: The F-distribution is a continuous distribution used in hypothesis testing for comparing the variances of two or more groups.

Understanding these common probability distributions and their properties is essential for conducting statistical analyses, making predictions, and drawing conclusions from data. These distributions form the foundation of inferential statistics.

Chapter Three

Sampling Distributions and Central Limit Theorem

7.1 Sampling Distributions

A sampling distribution is a theoretical distribution that describes the statistics (such as the mean or proportion) derived from multiple samples of the same size taken from a population. The concept of sampling distributions is crucial in statistical inference, where we make inferences about a population based on sample data.

7.2 Central Limit Theorem: Concept and Implications

The Central Limit Theorem (CLT) is a fundamental concept in statistics with profound implications for data analysis. It states the following:

Given a sufficiently large sample size (n) from a population with any shape of distribution, the sampling distribution of the sample mean will be approximately normally distributed.

Implications of the Central Limit Theorem:

- Regardless of the shape of the population distribution, the sampling distribution of the sample mean will tend to be normally distributed when the sample size is large enough.

- The larger the sample size, the closer the sampling distribution of the sample mean will be to a normal distribution.

- The mean of the sampling distribution of the sample mean will be equal to the population mean.

- The standard deviation of the sampling distribution of the sample mean, also known as the standard error of the mean (SEM), is equal to the population standard deviation divided by the

square root of the sample size
($\sigma/\sqrt{n}$).

The Central Limit Theorem is especially valuable in inferential statistics. It allows us to make assumptions about the behavior of sample statistics, such as the sample mean, even if we don't know the underlying population distribution. It also serves as the basis for constructing confidence intervals and conducting hypothesis tests.

7.3 Confidence Intervals

A confidence interval is a range of values within which we can be reasonably confident that the population parameter (such as the population mean or proportion) lies. It is a product of the Central Limit Theorem and is calculated based on the sample statistic (e.g., sample mean) and the standard error.

For example, a 95% confidence interval for the population mean implies that if we were to repeat the sampling process many times and construct 95% confidence intervals from each sample, approximately 95% of those intervals would contain the true population mean.

7.4 Margin of Error

The margin of error is the maximum amount by which a sample statistic (such as the sample mean) is likely to differ from the true population parameter. It is related to the confidence interval and is influenced by the sample size and variability of the data.

A larger sample size generally results in a smaller margin of error and a more precise estimate of the population parameter.

In conclusion, understanding sampling distributions and the Central Limit Theorem is essential for making inferences about populations based on sample data. These concepts allow statisticians to draw reliable conclusions and quantify the uncertainty associated with their estimates. In the following chapters, we will explore hypothesis testing, correlation analysis, and regression, which further expand our ability to analyze data and make informed decisions.

Hypothesis Testing

8.1 Formulating Hypotheses

Hypothesis testing is a statistical method used to make decisions or draw conclusions about a population based on sample data.

It involves setting up two competing hypotheses, the null hypothesis (H0) and the alternative hypothesis (Ha).

- Null Hypothesis (H0): The null hypothesis is a statement of no effect, no difference, or no relationship in the population. It represents the status quo or the absence of any effect being studied.

- Alternative Hypothesis (Ha): The alternative hypothesis is a statement that contradicts the null hypothesis and represents the researcher's claim or the presence of an effect, difference, or relationship in the population.

Hypotheses are typically formulated in terms of population parameters, such as population means or proportions.

8.2 Type I and Type II Errors

In hypothesis testing, there are two types of errors that can occur:

- Type I Error (False Positive): Occurs when we reject the null hypothesis when it is true. In other words, we mistakenly conclude that there is an effect or relationship in the population when there is none.

- Type II Error (False Negative): Occurs when we fail to reject the null hypothesis when it is false. In this case, we fail to detect an effect or relationship that actually exists in the population.

The probability of making a Type I error is denoted as α (alpha), and it is controlled by the significance level set for the test. The probability of making a Type II error is denoted as β (beta) and is influenced by factors such as the sample size and the effect size.

8.3 One-Sample and Two-Sample Tests

There are various types of hypothesis tests, each applicable to different scenarios:

- One-Sample Tests: These tests are used when we have one sample and want to compare the sample mean or proportion to a known value or hypothesized value. Examples include one-sample t-tests for means and one-sample proportion tests.

- Two-Sample Tests: These tests are used when we have two independent samples and want to compare the means or proportions between the two groups. Examples include two-sample t-tests for means and chi-square tests for proportions.

8.4 Paired and Independent Samples Tests

- Paired Samples Tests: Paired samples tests are used when we have two related samples, such as pre-test and post-test measurements on the same subjects. The paired t-test is commonly used in this scenario.

- Independent Samples Tests: Independent samples tests are used when we have two unrelated samples, and we want to compare their means or proportions. Examples include independent t-tests for means and chi-square tests for proportions.

8.5 ANOVA (Analysis of Variance)

ANOVA is a hypothesis testing method used to compare means among three or more groups. It helps determine if there are any significant differences in the population means. ANOVA tests the null hypothesis that all group means are equal.

If ANOVA indicates that there are significant differences among the group means, post-hoc tests, such as Tukey's HSD (honestly significant difference) or

Bonferroni corrections, can be conducted to identify which groups differ significantly from each other.

Hypothesis testing is a powerful tool for making data-driven decisions and drawing conclusions about populations based on sample data. Understanding the concept of hypothesis testing and the types of tests available enables researchers and analysts to conduct robust statistical analyses and provide evidence for their claims. In the following chapters, we will explore correlation analysis and regression, which allow us to examine relationships and make predictions using statistical models.

Correlation and Regression Analysis

9.1 Scatter Plots and Correlation Coefficient

Correlation analysis is used to study the relationship between two numerical variables. The first step in correlation analysis is to create a scatter plot, which visually represents the data points on a graph, with one variable on the x-axis and the other on the y-axis.

The correlation coefficient measures the strength and direction of the linear relationship between the two variables. It is denoted by the symbol "r" and ranges from -1 to +1. A positive value of "r" indicates a positive correlation (as one variable increases, the other tends to increase), while a negative value indicates a negative correlation (as one variable increases, the other tends to decrease). A correlation coefficient close to 0 suggests a weak or no linear relationship between the variables.

9.2 Simple Linear Regression

Simple linear regression is a statistical method used to model the relationship between two numerical variables when there is a linear association between them. It aims to find the best-fitting straight line (regression line) that minimizes the distance between the data points and the line.

The equation of the regression line is given by:

$$y = b0 + b1*x$$

Where:

- y is the dependent variable (the variable being predicted or explained).

- x is the independent variable (the predictor variable).

- b0 is the intercept (the value of y when x is 0).

- b1 is the slope (the change in y for a one-unit change in x).

The regression coefficients (b0 and b1) are estimated using the method of least squares, which minimizes the sum of the squared differences between the observed y values and the predicted values from the regression line.

9.3 Multiple Regression

Multiple regression extends simple linear regression to model the relationship between a dependent variable and two or more independent variables. It allows for the consideration of multiple predictors when explaining the variation in the dependent variable.

The multiple regression equation is given by:

y = b0 + b1*x1 + b2*x2 + ... + bn*xn

Where:

- y is the dependent variable.

- x1, x2, ..., xn are the independent variables.

- b0 is the intercept.

- b1, b2, ..., bn are the regression coefficients associated with each independent variable.

Multiple regression coefficients are estimated using similar least squares methods to find the best-fitting regression line.

9.4 Interpreting Regression Output

In regression analysis, the regression output provides valuable information about the model's goodness of fit, the significance of the predictors, and the overall predictive power of the model. Key elements of the output include the coefficient estimates, standard errors, p-values, and R-squared (or adjusted R-squared) values.

9.5 Residual Analysis

Residual analysis is performed to assess the model's assumptions and check for potential problems. Residuals are the differences between the observed y values and the predicted values from the regression line. A scatter plot of the residuals should show a random pattern with no obvious trends, indicating that the model assumptions are met.

Correlation and regression analysis allow researchers to

quantify and understand the relationships between variables, make predictions, and assess the importance of predictors in explaining variations in the dependent variable. They are widely used in various fields, such as economics, social sciences, finance, and marketing, to gain insights and make data-driven decisions.

Non-Parametric Methods

10.1 Introduction to Non-Parametric Methods

Non-parametric methods are a set of statistical techniques used when the underlying data distribution does not meet the assumptions of normality or when the population parameters are unknown. Unlike parametric methods that rely on specific assumptions about the data distribution, non-parametric methods make fewer assumptions and are more robust to deviations from normality.

Non-parametric methods are valuable in various scenarios, including when dealing with ordinal or categorical data, small sample sizes, outliers, or data that cannot be easily transformed into a normal distribution.

10.2 Mann-Whitney U Test (Wilcoxon Rank-Sum Test)

The Mann-Whitney U test is a non-parametric test used to compare the medians of two independent groups. It is an alternative to the independent two-sample t-test when the data do not meet the assumptions of normality.

The test involves converting the data into ranks, combining the ranks from both groups, and calculating the U statistic. The U statistic is used to assess whether there are significant differences between the groups.

10.3 Wilcoxon Signed-Rank Test

The Wilcoxon signed-rank test is a non-parametric test used to compare the medians of paired or matched samples. It is employed when the data are not normally distributed or when the data points are related.

The test involves computing the differences between the paired data, converting them into ranks (ignoring zero differences), and calculating the signed-rank statistic. The signed-rank statistic is then used to determine if there are significant differences between the paired samples.

10.4 Kruskal-Wallis Test

The Kruskal-Wallis test is a non-parametric test used to compare three or more independent groups. It is an extension of the Mann-Whitney U test for multiple groups.

The test ranks all data points from all groups, calculates the sum of ranks for each group, and then computes the Kruskal-Wallis H statistic. The H statistic is used to determine if there are significant differences between the groups.

10.5 Spearman's Rank Correlation

Spearman's rank correlation is a non-parametric measure of the strength and direction of the monotonic relationship between two variables. It is used when the variables do not have a linear relationship or when the data are ordinal or ranked.

Spearman's rank correlation involves converting the data into ranks and then calculating the correlation coefficient (rho) based on the ranks. The coefficient ranges from -1 to +1, where -1 indicates a perfect negative monotonic relationship, +1 indicates a perfect positive monotonic relationship, and 0 indicates no monotonic relationship.

10.6 Chi-Square Test for Independence

The chi-square test for independence is a non-parametric test used to determine if there is a significant association between two categorical variables. It is used when both variables have discrete categories and are not normally distributed.

The test involves creating a contingency table, which cross-tabulates the frequencies of the two variables. The chi-square statistic is then calculated based on the differences between the observed and expected frequencies. The chi-square statistic is compared to the critical value from the chi-square distribution to determine if there is a significant association between the variables.

Non-parametric methods provide valuable alternatives to parametric tests when the assumptions of normality and parametric statistics are not met. They are versatile and widely used in various fields, especially in situations where data may not adhere to strict distributional assumptions. By using non-parametric methods, researchers can draw robust conclusions and make informed decisions even with non-normally distributed data. In the following chapters, we will delve into experimental design and Bayesian statistics, which offer additional tools for hypothesis testing and decision-making in various contexts.

Chapter Four

Experimental Design and Analysis

11.1 Introduction to Experimental Design

Experimental design is a structured and systematic approach to planning and conducting experiments. It is a crucial step in the scientific method, helping researchers control and manipulate variables to investigate cause-and-effect relationships and draw valid conclusions. Well-designed experiments provide reliable and interpretable results.

11.2 Control Groups and Randomization

Two fundamental principles in experimental design are the use of control groups and randomization:

- Control Group: A control group is a group in an experiment that receives no treatment or a standard treatment. It serves as a baseline for comparison to assess the effect of the experimental intervention. By comparing the treatment group with the control group, researchers can isolate the treatment effect from other confounding factors.

- Randomization: Randomization involves assigning participants or subjects to different treatment groups randomly. Randomization helps ensure that the groups are similar and that any differences observed between them are likely due to the treatment rather than biases in group assignment.

11.3 Between-Subjects and Within-Subjects Designs

Experimental designs can be classified into between-subjects and within-subjects designs:

- Between-Subjects Design: In a between-subjects design, different groups of participants are exposed to different treatments or conditions. Each group is independent, and the responses are compared between the groups. Between-subjects designs are useful when there is a risk of carry-over effects or when participants cannot be exposed to multiple conditions.

- Within-Subjects Design: In a within-subjects design (also known as repeated measures design), each participant is exposed to all treatment conditions. The same participants act as their control group, reducing individual variability and increasing statistical power.

Within-subjects designs are efficient but may suffer from order effects.

11.4 Factorial Design

Factorial design is a type of experimental design that involves studying the effects of two or more independent variables simultaneously. The different combinations of the independent variables create various conditions, allowing researchers to explore interactions between factors.

For example, in a 2x2 factorial design, there are two independent variables, each with two levels. This results in four different conditions. Factorial designs are powerful for investigating main effects and interactions between variables.

11.5 Analysis of Variance (ANOVA)

Analysis of Variance (ANOVA) is a statistical technique used to compare means among three or more groups. ANOVA tests the null hypothesis that all group means are equal. If the null hypothesis is rejected, post-hoc tests (e.g., Tukey's HSD or Bonferroni corrections) can identify which groups differ significantly.

ANOVA is widely used in experimental research and can be applied to both between-subjects and within-subjects designs.

11.6 Randomized Controlled Trials (RCTs)

Randomized Controlled Trials (RCTs) are a type of experimental design commonly used in medical, social, and psychological research. RCTs randomly assign participants to different treatment groups and control groups to evaluate the efficacy of interventions or treatments.

RCTs are considered the gold standard for assessing causal

relationships, as randomization helps eliminate selection bias and ensures that the groups are comparable.

11.7 Quasi-Experimental Designs

Quasi-experimental designs are similar to experimental designs but lack random assignment to treatment groups. These designs are often used when randomization is not feasible or ethical.

While quasi-experimental designs may not establish causality as strongly as true experiments, they can still provide valuable insights into the effects of interventions or treatments.

Experimental design is a powerful tool for investigating cause-and-effect relationships and drawing valid conclusions. By implementing control groups, randomization, and well-designed experimental structures, researchers can conduct rigorous experiments that contribute to scientific knowledge and inform evidence-based decision-making.

Bayesian Statistics

12.1 Introduction to Bayesian Statistics

Bayesian statistics is a branch of statistics that provides a different approach to statistical inference compared to classical or frequentist statistics. While classical statistics relies on probability distributions of data given the parameters (data | parameters), Bayesian statistics focuses on the probability distributions of parameters given the data (parameters | data).

Bayesian statistics incorporates prior knowledge or beliefs about the parameters and updates them using observed data to obtain posterior probability distributions. It provides a framework for quantifying uncertainty, making predictions, and incorporating new information into the analysis.

12.2 Bayes' Theorem in Bayesian Statistics

At the core of Bayesian statistics is Bayes' theorem, which relates the prior probability of an event (prior belief) to its posterior probability (updated belief) after considering new evidence. Bayes' theorem is expressed as:

P(parameters | data) = [P(data | parameters) * P(parameters)] / P(data)

Where:

- P(parameters | data) is the posterior probability of the parameters given the data.

- P(data | parameters) is the likelihood of the data given the parameters.

- P(parameters) is the prior probability of the parameters (prior belief).

- P(data) is the marginal likelihood of the data (normalizing constant).

12.3 Prior and Posterior Distributions

The prior distribution represents the initial beliefs or knowledge about the parameters before observing any data. It can be based on previous studies, expert opinions, or other sources of information.

After observing the data, the prior distribution is combined with the likelihood function (representing the probability of the data given the parameters) to obtain the posterior distribution. The posterior distribution reflects the updated beliefs about the parameters after incorporating the new evidence from the data.

12.4 Markov Chain Monte Carlo (MCMC) Methods

In Bayesian statistics, direct computation of the posterior distribution is often challenging or intractable, especially for complex models. Markov Chain Monte Carlo (MCMC) methods are a family of computational techniques used to approximate the posterior distribution.

MCMC methods, such as the Metropolis-Hastings algorithm and Gibbs sampling, generate a sequence of samples from the posterior distribution. These samples can be used to estimate posterior summary statistics or construct credible intervals for the parameters.

12.5 Bayesian vs. Frequentist Approach

The Bayesian and frequentist approaches to statistical inference have some fundamental differences:

- Interpretation of Probability: In Bayesian statistics, probability is a measure of uncertainty and represents subjective beliefs or degrees of belief. In frequentist statistics, probability is solely based on the long-run frequency of events in repeated experiments.

- Handling of Parameters: In Bayesian statistics, parameters are treated as random variables, and their uncertainty is quantified through probability distributions. In frequentist statistics, parameters are fixed but unknown, and estimates are obtained using point estimates and confidence intervals.

- Incorporation of Prior Information: Bayesian statistics allows for the incorporation of prior information or beliefs about the parameters, whereas frequentist statistics does not consider prior information.

12.6 Bayesian Applications

Bayesian statistics has applications in various fields, including:

- Parameter Estimation: Bayesian methods provide credible intervals and posterior distributions for parameters.

- Hypothesis Testing: Bayesian hypothesis testing involves comparing posterior probabilities of different hypotheses.

- Bayesian Regression: Bayesian regression models allow for uncertainty quantification in regression analysis.

- Bayesian Decision Analysis: Bayesian decision analysis helps in decision-making under uncertainty, incorporating costs and utilities.

- Machine Learning: Bayesian methods are used in machine learning for probabilistic modeling, Bayesian networks, and hierarchical models.

Bayesian statistics offers a powerful framework for handling uncertainty, incorporating prior knowledge, and making predictions. It is particularly valuable in situations with limited data or when there is a need to update beliefs as new data becomes available. By embracing Bayesian methods, researchers can gain a deeper understanding of their data and make more informed decisions in a wide range of applications.

Time Series Analysis

13.1 Introduction to Time Series Analysis

Time series analysis is a statistical method used to analyze and model data that are collected over time. In a time series, observations are recorded at regular intervals, forming a sequence of data points. Time series data often exhibit patterns, trends, seasonality, and other structures that make them different from cross-sectional or independent data.

Time series analysis aims to understand and model these patterns, make predictions about future values, and extract valuable insights from the data.

13.2 Components of Time Series

A time series can be decomposed into several components:

- Trend: The long-term movement or direction in the data over time. It represents the underlying pattern that may increase or decrease over time.

- Seasonality: The recurring and predictable patterns that repeat at fixed intervals within a time series. Seasonal patterns might be daily, weekly, monthly, or seasonal.

- Cyclic Variation: The fluctuating patterns that are not regular like seasonality but occur over extended periods and do not repeat at fixed intervals.

- Irregular (Random) Variation: The residual or random noise left after removing the trend, seasonality, and cyclic components. It represents the unpredictable and random variations in the data.

13.3 Time Series Visualization

Visualizing time series data is essential to identify patterns and gain insights. Common techniques include:

- Line Plots: Line plots are simple graphs that display the time series data as a line connecting data points at each time step.

- Seasonal Subseries Plots: Seasonal subseries plots break down the data into smaller seasonal periods and plot them separately to visualize seasonal patterns.

- Box Plots: Box plots show the distribution of the data at different time steps, helping to identify potential outliers or unusual patterns.

13.4 Time Series Modeling

Time series modeling involves developing mathematical models that represent the underlying patterns in the data. The goal is to capture the trend, seasonality, and other components to make predictions and forecast future values.

- Autoregressive Integrated Moving Average (ARIMA): ARIMA is a popular time series model that combines autoregressive (AR), differencing (I), and moving average (MA) components to handle stationary time series data.

- Seasonal ARIMA (SARIMA): SARIMA extends ARIMA to handle seasonal time series by incorporating seasonal components.

- Exponential Smoothing Models: Exponential smoothing models use weighted averages of past observations to forecast future values. Examples include Simple Exponential Smoothing, Holt's Linear Exponential Smoothing, and Holt-Winters Exponential Smoothing for seasonality.

13.5 Time Series Forecasting

Time series forecasting is the process of predicting future values based on past data. Forecasting can be achieved using various time series models, and the choice of the model depends on the specific characteristics of the data.

Forecasting methods include:

- One-Step-Ahead Forecasting: Making predictions one step into the future based on the current and past observations.

- Multi-Step Forecasting: Making predictions several steps into the future, often using iterative approaches.

- Rolling Forecast: Updating the model at each time step and making predictions for a fixed number of future steps.

13.6 Evaluating Forecasting Accuracy

To assess the accuracy of time series forecasts, various metrics are used, including:

- Mean Absolute Error (MAE): The average absolute difference between the actual and forecasted values.

- Root Mean Squared Error (RMSE): The square root of the average of the squared differences between actual and forecasted values.

- Mean Absolute Percentage Error (MAPE): The percentage difference between actual and forecasted values.

- Forecast Error Variance Decomposition (FEVD): Decomposing the forecast error variance into contributions from different components.

Time series analysis and forecasting are critical in various fields, such as finance, economics, sales forecasting, weather forecasting, and many others. By analyzing time series data, researchers and analysts can uncover patterns, make informed predictions, and make better decisions based on the historical trends and patterns observed in the data.

Chapter Five

Introduction to Statistical Software

14.1 Overview of Statistical Software

Statistical software is a specialized type of computer software designed to perform statistical analysis, data manipulation, and data visualization. These software tools are essential for researchers, analysts, and professionals working in various fields to analyze data, make data-driven decisions, and draw insights from complex datasets.

Statistical software provides a wide range of functionalities, from basic descriptive statistics to advanced modeling and simulation techniques. They often come with user-friendly interfaces and programming capabilities to cater to both non-technical users and experienced statisticians.

14.2 Common Statistical Software

There are several popular statistical software packages available, each with its strengths and focus areas:

- R: R is an open-source programming language and environment specifically designed for statistical computing and graphics. It has a vast collection of packages contributed by the R community, making it highly extensible and versatile for a wide range of statistical analyses.

- Python: Python is a general-purpose programming language with various libraries for data manipulation, analysis, and visualization. The most prominent library for statistical computing in Python is pandas, and additional packages like NumPy, SciPy, and statsmodels provide additional statistical functionalities.

- SPSS: SPSS (Statistical Package for the Social Sciences) is a widely used software suite for statistical analysis and data management. It is particularly popular in social sciences research and offers both a graphical user interface and a syntax-based interface.

- Stata: Stata is a powerful statistical software package used for data analysis, data management, and graphics. It is widely used in the social sciences, health research, and economics.

- SAS: SAS (Statistical Analysis System) is a comprehensive software suite for advanced statistical analysis, business intelligence, and data management. It is widely used in various industries, including healthcare, finance, and market research.

- Excel: While not exclusively a statistical software, Microsoft Excel is a widely accessible tool that includes basic statistical functions and tools for data analysis.

14.3 Capabilities of Statistical Software

Statistical software provides a broad range of capabilities, including:

- Data Import and Manipulation: Importing data from various

formats, cleaning and transforming data, and preparing data for analysis.

- Descriptive Statistics: Calculating summary statistics such as mean, median, standard deviation, and other measures of central tendency and dispersion.

- Inferential Statistics: Conducting hypothesis tests, estimating parameters, and performing analysis of variance (ANOVA).

- Regression Analysis: Performing simple and multiple regression, logistic regression, time series regression, and nonlinear regression.

- Data Visualization: Creating various charts, plots, and graphs to visualize data distributions and relationships.

- Time Series Analysis: Analyzing time series data, detecting trends, seasonality, and forecasting future values.

- Bayesian Analysis: Implementing Bayesian methods for parameter estimation, prediction, and decision-making under uncertainty.

- Machine Learning: Applying machine learning algorithms for classification, regression, clustering, and other data-driven tasks.

14.4 Choosing the Right Statistical Software

When choosing statistical software, consider factors such as:

- Functionality: Assess the software's capabilities and whether it meets your specific needs for data analysis and modeling.

- Ease of Use: Consider the user interface and the learning curve associated with the software. Some tools may be more suitable for non-technical users, while others require programming knowledge.

- Community Support: Check the availability of user forums, documentation, and online resources to get assistance and support when needed.

- Cost: Evaluate the pricing and licensing options, especially for commercial software packages.

- Integration: Consider whether the software can integrate with other tools and systems used in your organization.

The choice of statistical software ultimately depends on your specific requirements, familiarity with programming languages, and the complexity of the analyses you need to perform. Each software package has its unique advantages and disadvantages, so it is worth exploring different options to find the one that best suits your needs.

Ethics in Statistics

15.1 Importance of Ethics in Statistics

Ethics in statistics refers to the principles and guidelines that govern the responsible and ethical conduct of statistical practices. As statistics play a significant role in decision-making, policy formulation, and scientific research, it is crucial to ensure that statistical analyses are conducted with integrity, transparency, and respect for the rights and welfare of individuals and populations.

Ethical considerations in statistics are essential to uphold the credibility and validity of research findings, protect the rights and privacy of human subjects, and maintain the public's trust in the scientific community.

15.2 Ethical Principles in Statistics

Several ethical principles guide the responsible practice of statistics:

- Honesty and Integrity: Researchers and statisticians must be honest and transparent in their work, accurately reporting their findings and avoiding any misrepresentation of data or results.

- Objectivity and Impartiality: Statistical analyses should be conducted impartially and without bias, regardless of the desired outcome or preferences of stakeholders.

- Informed Consent: When involving human subjects in research, informed consent is crucial. Participants should be fully informed about the study's purpose, procedures, potential risks, and their rights before giving consent to participate.

- Privacy and Confidentiality: Statisticians must protect the privacy and confidentiality of individuals whose data is being analyzed. Data should be anonymized and only used for the specific purposes outlined in the informed consent.

- Responsible Data Handling: Statisticians must handle data

responsibly, ensuring data security, accuracy, and proper storage. Data should be used only for legitimate research purposes.

- Avoiding Harm: Researchers should consider the potential risks and benefits of their studies and take measures to minimize harm to participants and society.

15.3 Reproducibility and Transparency

Reproducibility and transparency are essential aspects of ethical statistical practice:

- Reproducibility: Researchers should ensure that their analyses are reproducible, meaning that others can replicate their findings using the same data and methods. This promotes scientific accountability and fosters trust in research outcomes.

- Transparency: Researchers should provide clear and detailed documentation of their methodologies, data sources, and analytical procedures. Transparency allows others to assess the validity and reliability of the results.

15.4 Data Manipulation and Misconduct

Data manipulation and scientific misconduct are serious ethical breaches in statistics:

- Data Fabrication: Inventing or falsifying data is a severe form of scientific misconduct and undermines the integrity of research.

- Data Cherry-Picking: Selectively choosing or omitting data to support a particular hypothesis or conclusion is unethical and distorts the true picture of the data.

- Publication Bias: Failing to publish negative or inconclusive results can lead to publication bias, which skews the scientific literature and impedes scientific progress.

- Plagiarism: Presenting others' work or ideas as one's own, without proper attribution, is unethical and a breach of academic integrity.

15.5 Ethical Review and Institutional Oversight

In many research settings, particularly when human subjects are involved, an ethical review by an Institutional Review Board (IRB) or Ethics Committee is necessary. The IRB ensures that research involving human participants meets ethical standards and safeguards participants' rights and welfare.

15.6 Responsible Communication of Findings

Ethical responsibility extends to the communication of statistical findings:

- Avoiding Overinterpretation: Researchers should present their results accurately and avoid overinterpretation or exaggeration of findings.

- Openness to Critique: Researchers should welcome critiques and constructive feedback from their peers to strengthen the quality of their work.

- Acknowledgment of Limitations: Researchers should acknowledge the limitations of their studies and be transparent about uncertainties.

15.7 Ethical Challenges in Big Data and AI

With the advent of big data and artificial intelligence (AI), new ethical challenges have emerged in data collection, analysis, and decision-making. Issues related to data privacy, algorithmic bias, and the use of AI in sensitive areas require careful ethical considerations and responsible practices.

Adhering to ethical principles in statistics is essential for maintaining the credibility of research, protecting individuals' rights, and ensuring that the knowledge generated through statistical analyses contributes positively to society. By upholding ethical standards, statisticians and researchers can build trust with the public, policymakers, and other stakeholders and promote the responsible use of data-driven insights.

Conclusion

16.1 The Role of Statistics in Decision Making

The role of statistics in decision-making is of paramount importance, as it provides a systematic and objective approach to analyzing data and making informed choices. Statistics allows decision-makers to:

1. Data Collection and Analysis: Statistics helps in collecting relevant data from various sources, organizing it, and summarizing it in a meaningful way. By analyzing data using

statistical methods, decision-makers can identify trends, patterns, and relationships that inform their understanding of the situation.

2. Quantifying Uncertainty: In many decision-making scenarios, there is inherent uncertainty. Statistics provides tools to quantify uncertainty through measures like confidence intervals and probability distributions. Decision-makers can assess the range of possible outcomes and associated risks, enabling them to make more informed choices.

3. Comparing Alternatives: Decision-making often involves evaluating different alternatives or options. Statistics enables the comparison of these alternatives by providing methods like hypothesis testing, analysis of variance, and regression analysis. These techniques help identify significant differences and relationships between variables, aiding in the decision-making process.

4. Forecasting and Predictive Analytics: Time series analysis and predictive modeling allow decision-makers to forecast future trends and outcomes

based on historical data. This information helps in planning, resource allocation, and risk management.

5. Quality Control and Process Improvement: Statistics plays a vital role in quality control and process improvement initiatives. Tools like control charts and process capability analysis help monitor and enhance the quality of products or services, leading to better decision-making for process optimization.

6. Sampling Techniques: In situations where collecting data from the entire population is impractical or costly, statistics

offers various sampling techniques that allow decision-makers to draw valid conclusions from a representative sample of the population.

7. Business Analytics: In the business world, statistical methods are widely used in market research, customer segmentation, demand forecasting, and pricing optimization. By analyzing data, businesses can gain valuable insights to improve their products, services, and overall performance.

8. Public Policy and Governance: Statistics plays a crucial role in

shaping public policies and governance decisions. Data-driven policies are more likely to be evidence-based and effective in addressing societal challenges, such as healthcare allocation, education initiatives, and economic planning.

9. Risk Assessment and Management: Statistics is used in risk assessment and risk management to estimate the probability of adverse events occurring and their potential impact. This information helps decision-makers develop appropriate strategies to mitigate

risks and protect against uncertainties.

10. Healthcare and Medicine: In the medical field, statistics is instrumental in clinical trials, epidemiological studies, and healthcare outcomes analysis. It helps healthcare professionals make informed decisions about treatments, interventions, and patient care.

In essence, statistics provides decision-makers with a powerful set of tools to analyze data, draw conclusions, and make evidence-based choices. By embracing statistical techniques and principles, decision-makers can enhance their ability to solve complex problems, optimize processes, and achieve better outcomes across various domains, ultimately leading to more informed and successful decision-making.

16.2 Continuous Learning and Further Exploration

Continuous learning and further exploration in the field of statistics are essential for personal and professional growth. The field of statistics is dynamic, and new methodologies, techniques, and applications emerge regularly. To stay current and make meaningful contributions, individuals interested in statistics should consider the following:

1. Stay Updated with the Latest Developments: Subscribe to statistical journals, attend conferences, and participate in workshops or webinars to stay informed about the latest research, advancements, and trends in statistics.

2. Learn New Statistical Software and Programming Languages: Familiarity with various statistical software (e.g., R, Python, SAS) and programming languages (e.g., SQL, MATLAB) can enhance analytical capabilities and open

up new opportunities for data analysis.

3. Engage in Data Analysis Projects: Engaging in real-world data analysis projects allows individuals to apply statistical concepts to practical scenarios, gaining hands-on experience and problem-solving skills.

4. Explore Specialized Areas: Statistics encompasses various specialized areas, such as Bayesian statistics, machine learning, spatial statistics, and biostatistics. Exploring these areas deepens expertise and opens doors to diverse career opportunities.

5. Seek Advanced Education:
Pursuing advanced degrees or
certifications in statistics or
related fields provides a strong
foundation and credibility for a
career in data analysis and
research.

6. Contribute to Open-Source
Projects: Participating in open-
source statistical software
projects or contributing to
statistical communities fosters
collaboration, knowledge sharing,
and networking with other
statisticians.

7. Collaborate with Experts from
Different Disciplines:
Collaborating with experts from

diverse fields exposes statisticians to new perspectives, challenges, and data types, expanding their horizons and problem-solving abilities.

8. Read Books and Online Resources: There are numerous books, online courses, and tutorials available for further exploration and learning in statistics. Utilize these resources to deepen knowledge in specific topics of interest.

9. Join Professional Organizations: Joining statistical or data science professional organizations provide access to networking opportunities,

conferences, and educational resources.

10. Practice Ethical Conduct: Emphasize ethical considerations in statistical analysis and research, ensuring data integrity, transparency, and responsible data handling.

Continuous learning and exploration are vital for remaining at the forefront of statistical practice and innovation. As the field evolves, statisticians who embrace ongoing learning are better equipped to tackle complex challenges, contribute to cutting-edge research, and make a positive impact in various industries and domains. By cultivating a passion for statistics and a commitment to growth, individuals can thrive in the ever-evolving world of data analysis and decision-making.